D1240907

Also by Naomi Feigelson Chase

THE JUDGE'S DAUGHTER

NAOMI FEIGELSON CHASE

Acknowledgements

Sections of this poem have appeared in Sojourner and won an award from the Judah Magnes Museum.

The author wishes to thank the MacDowell Colony and Yaddo where parts of this poem where written.

Cover photo by Doris Ellenbogen
Cover design by Linda Burns
ISBN 1-882329-07-4
Library of Congress Catalogue Card No.: 95-078486
Published by Garden Street Press
PO Box 1231
Truro, Massachusetts 02666

To my Baba and Zadi, Gertrude and Nathan Savage

I sit backwards on the toilet while mother braids my hair,

on Pocusset Street, upstairs from the Marks.

Jeanette teaches me to knit army scarves that wind

around the house. Saturdays, pick-up sticks with Dr. Wein,

the neurosurgeon next door. I picture him tickling

inside his patients' heads with purple tipped wands.

Jeanette's black Scotty runs away

in his plaid coat, then comes home.

My mother sat home in arctic darkness; my father,
in black court robes, dispensing law. My footsteps echoed
down long marble corridors, past shirt-sleeved men hoping
to get their sons a policeman's job.
Oyey, Oyey. All stood till father sat, pounding
a gavel, the kind Aunt Eva flattened veal with.
At school, we stood for the teacher in stiff pleated uniforms.
In my notebook, I drew seated Egyptian Queens.

I didn't know steel was made
in white-hot furnaces, by half-naked,
sweating men called *Hunkies, Polacks.*
At night, in bed, I saw their fires
reflected in a metal sky.
I read, tunneling
under blankets with a flashlight,
dreamed of fires burning underground.

In Washington, when he was in Roosevelt's Congress.

Father said goodnight to me

on the radio.

My parents gave parties,

white silk mother,

flowers on her bared shoulder.

Upstairs I cut half moons in my pajamas

with father's cuticle scissors.

My parents never touched each other, only things.

Mother's solitaire cards, father's newspapers,

ivory he collected:

a Japanese lady with black pompadours,

tiny reindeer pulling a tiny ice sled.

Mother's picture albums:

father and mother faded brown

in the Philippines;

Banff, mother in a three-cornered hat,

father in knickers,

me

in a vanilla dress

with a big brown collar,

on the steps

of the Baltimore three-family

where mother lived as a girl.

Mother bought old, broken chairs

for Miss Gregorian,

her red lipsticked mouth filled

with carpet tacks. She stuck

the chairs with squares of embroidered roses,

sewed across the rugs on her knees,

trailing thread.

I stroked the roses.

At night, afraid of dying

I couldn't sleep,

once poured water

on my sheets,

told my parents I'd wet my bed

and had to sleep with them.

Father put towels

on the sheets.

In 1918, after my father's father's appendix burst

and he turned black and died, grandmother ruined

his dry goods business. She gave up Vienna, maids and carriage,

brought her lace gowns and my father to Pittsburgh

and opened a boarding house. The frown in her face

started when she broke her daughter Dora's arm,

for marrying at eighteen, for being beautiful,

my grandmother still a widow.

Father scraped the German off his tongue

with stones, like the Greek

who learned to speak

with pebbles in his mouth.

He walked down Pocusset Street spitting pebbles,

practicing the speech from Coriolanus,

how the parts of the body

are like the body politic.

All father's family who hadn't died in ovens

came to Pittsburgh,

Adolph, the bartender,

Ted, the lawyer,

Peppy, the accountant,

cousin Leisl

whom I hated

for her dolls, their luggage, their hand-made clothes.

I stole a doll dress.

Father threatened,

"Next time, jail."

Peppy and father

each claimed

he rescued Dora, the photographer,

her cameras

and her fourth husband.

Father's bailiff, Penrose, combed

scant hairs with his fingers,

blinked before

he swore in the criminals.

Life, gaveled father.

Paula, his secretary,

filed prisoners

in steel drawers.

At night the convicts took my bed.

I walked the dungeon,

hands 'cuffed back.

I'd do my time.

When I got out,

like Bogart,

I'd go to a doctor

and get a new face.

Father's breakfast: two soft boiled

egg whites, hot water,

blackstrap molasses,

unfortified yogurt,

wheat germ,

Vitamin C, Vitamin E.

A small blue glass of green liqueur

after court.

My parents went to Japan on a Congressional junket.

I went to *Baba* and *Zadi*. *Baba* taught me cooking

and politics: where to spy *Pesach chomitz* , how

to hold the wooden bowl against my chest and chop, why

honey for *tzimmes,*

why it's better to picket than pray.

Zadi held me on his lap to cry

when Mimi died in the radio opera.

In high school, mother worked in the Five and Ten.

She liked silk, velvet ribbons,

the names: *piquet, bombazine, rickrack;*

measuring cloth on long wood rulers,

cutting with saw-toothed scissors,

winding silk

around her fingers

like rings.

My mother read Borges,

told me of a man

who found the *Aleph*

at the bottom

of the basement stairs.

With patience, I'd find it.

So I sat

and waited.

When mother got sick

she went away

to take the waters,

kneeled

at the water's edge,

draining the sea.

She came home

and rooms got dark again.

My mother murders me.

I open the bathroom door and watch.

She unlaces her stiff pink corset

and her breasts fall out.

She takes a hard-tipped lace,

puts it around my throat ,

and pulls.

"Go away," she says. "Take your life."

In the dark, mother dreamed father young,

cursed her brother for introducing them

when she was beautiful and didn't know it.

She's three in Vilna. Her mother,

in something long and dark, buttons my mother's smock.

They're off to America, where *Zadi* went in hay,

hiding from Cossacks. If she's good,

soon she'll see her father.

Maude, the nurse, came when I was eight, just before

Sarah was born. I wanted Maude for me.

One night as she rocked Sarah in our room,

I rose from bed, eyes closed,

shook my wrists, wiggled my hips,

moaned.

Maude put Sarah down. Kissed me to bed.

"White folks," she said.

Mother took me to ballet

with women who were swans

and swam on their toes.

I took tap

after Sarah was born

and I got fat,

an elephant

with metal feet.

"You're going to jail," Father said.

Kate, the new maid, pretended

to fix breakfast.

"You told on me. I'll tell you slap

me and pinch Sarah."

"Who'd believe a criminal?" she said.

The courtroom,

me in the witness box,

Father in robes,

banged the gavel.

"In Kate's room, stealing."

Banged the gavel.

I said, "She hits me with a spatula."

"Guilty, with an explanation."

I said, "She pinches Sarah."

"Prisoner paroled to her home."

Ten ways to get rid of Sarah:

Cook her in chicken soup.

Bury her in a sand castle.

Donate her tushy to science.

Drop her off Steel Pier.

Sell her to kidnappers.

Rub her together with two sticks.

Play doctor and

operate on her.

Put her out

with the garbage.

Mail her

to relatives in Russia.

Feed her,

feed her,

feed her.

Bloomers for hockey

in Winchester School for Girls.

Always thwacked, never scored.

I relished forbidden

Christian songs, saints

throwing golden crowns

before a glassy sea.

Or was it "grassy?"

I read Caesar's *Gallic Wars,* the *Aeneid,*

no "dirty" Latin poetry.

Mrs. Wills tried to expel me for arguing

Roosevelt wasn't a "Commie."

Good. I could go to school with boys

and wear real clothes.

They backed down for father: power

pulls harder than gravity.

I was sitting on the back porch

when the door slammed on the next Ventnor stoop

and Morton Gurevich, red curls and freckles,

took the stage. "How about the beach?"

just like that. "I'm not allowed."

He said, "Your social class makes you a prisoner.

My parents are Communists,

I'm going to be a stand-up comedian, entertain the masses."

We played

acey-deucey,

blind man's buff,

Jacks,

strip poker,

Old Maid,

bourgeois family,

barefoot doctor.

"Guns?" I asked. "What are they protecting us for?"

"From, not for," father said.

They slouched outside in black suits, hats.

Mother thought they might take out

porch furniture. "That's not why they're here," Father said.

Laura, the new maid, claimed a man father jailed

for murder was going to murder him.

"Nonsense, no one's killing me," father said.

They watched from the porch all summer

in their hats, smoking, drinking

mother's iced tea. I sat in the driveway

in the orange and green striped chair,

in my blue bathing suit,

reading, smelling of coconut oil.

If someone is going to shoot me,

let's get it over with.

For my thirteenth birthday, I got New York:

"Member of the Wedding,"

"The Confidential Clerk." Wanting to be T. S. Eliot,

more like left-out Frankie,

I got my first period at Sardis.

At the table, sure everyone was staring,

I forked a poached egg over my hash,

loaded on ketchup.

My parents argued

who would carry

father's tripod.

Mother did.

The night before we docked at Naples,

I tried to lose my virginity

with a steward,

but the lifeboats were full.

Capri was white walls with scarlet bougainvillea

I wanted to lick like a bee.

At Hotel Splendide, Faroukh, who'd just lost Egypt,

ate his way through exile.

Now only waiters bowed to him,

only one woman peeled his figs.

My mother said that waitressing is woman's lot;

my father, that it's hard to be a king.

I envied the switchboard operators

connecting worlds

in the telephone building,

Athena's Temple copied on Pocusset Street.

I wanted to call Athena in Greek,

speak to my Vilna relatives — if there were any left.

I wanted to ring up Dido, urge her

to avoid traveling men,

and not burn up for love.

My mother is on her knees,

scrubbing the kitchen floor.

She says, "It's my life," and puts newspapers to dry it.

She eats rye bread smeared with butter, ice cream with

sherbet before bed. Later, in the nursing home,

I'd bring her pastrami sandwiches with pickles, hot fudge

sundaes with whipped cream and nuts.

Anything sweet, anything sour.

Mother took walks with Sarah and me, holding

each with one hand, whispering in our ears how father

broke her heart, the heart she had in college, the one

she inked and wrote poems with, poems that burned

in a fire. I thought her real heart lay in a trunk upstairs

in tissue, between two kimonos she got in Japan

and never wore,

one jade-green, one peacock blue.

"Loud," she whispered. "Common, like me."

Mother, listening to flowers,

red nails pulling leaves

from her flowered house dress, pointing

to marigolds she planted by the garage.

"I hear them screaming."

I asked her, "What do they say?"

"Scream," she corrected, "plague,

I will drown fleeing Egypt. Ten years of bad luck."

Later, in the nursing home, she spoke

two words a year.

Couldn't or wouldn't,

we didn't know.

When the nuns walked her

between them, in the garden,

"More water," she said.

My mother got smaller and smaller.

I looked for her in corners, between fringes

of oriental rugs.

She rode out in a wheelchair,

a life-size cripple, bound by the belt

of her flowered house dress, the laces

of her black oxfords, her pink corset strings.

She rode around the house for years.

In the library, Athena greets me

from the porch of her marble doll house.

I offer gold raisins, silver twigs

for her temple fire.

At night I bring a ladder to let her out.

Barefoot, in her toga, she shows me

her pictures in books: Goddess of Sulfur and Brimstone,

Virgin, Goddess Who Came from Herself.

"Your life is on fire," she says. "Take it."